What We Are Given

ೞ

poems by Ollie O'Neill

Write Bloody UK

www.writebloodyuk.co.uk

First edition.
ISBN: 978-1838033200

Cover Design by Luna aït Oumeghar
Interior Layout by Winona León
Edited by Fern Angel Beattie and Wes Mongo Jolley
Proofread by Wes Mongo Jolley
Author Photo by Kit Sinclair

Type set in Bergamo.

Write Bloody UK
London, UK

Support Independent Presses
writebloodyuk.co.uk

For Talia Tosun
You loved to have the last word. Now the first one is for you, too.

WHAT WE ARE GIVEN

WHAT WE ARE GIVEN

Everyone I Love Is Capable of Dying

Everyone I love is capable of dying and I am in love with this fact, how unflinching it is, how lucky I am to be able to prepare for at least one abandonment. Nothing is sexier than the prospect of being left, and the dead do leaving so well. Love's appeal is in its propensity to end in heartbreak. What you can do before that is magical — eat mango from the navel of a woman who will break you, romance someone in the frozen food aisle. What is love for if not ruining basic experiences alongside someone else?

I want to love someone so hard I can barely be without remembering them.

Is It Harder to Be a Mother or a Daughter?

Grease spits and licks the tiled wall   wet knife between us

recently I cannot stop imagining   a future in which   I am both

in every version I am   the colour of the sun setting

somewhere in my body   palms cut up   from trying to hold back

the clock hands   she turns up uninvited   morning mirror

remember   when the doctor fit the cannula   pre-empted the flood

how we were seconds away from the water   carrying the patients

off the operating table   a river where there should never   be a river

remember how she slipped out   quiet as that first relapse

wedding song with a sweet lodged   in its throat   if a ghost enters a room

but nobody ever notices   can you still call the place haunted?

You've never been both   pushing dinner round the pan she says

all you know is taking   care   in our language originates from the Old High

German 'charon'   – to grieve   she turns the hob off   sudden quiet

where there used to be flames   readies a plate   asks me :

are you not even going to say thank you?

Oi When You Get This Call Me Please

One more dream in which she has already died
so I am repentant upon waking — a text
just to see her read it. An excuseless phone call
to cleanse a premature grief.

Memories are their own kind of affirmation.
I watch a home video, her mouth laughing
into the shape of her sister's name, eyes
already making promises.

Before I know the hospital has a ban on flowers
(something about germs, or the inevitable fate of each bunch)
I'm making small talk with the florist. Want to ask
about funerals without committing myself to a future.

Sometimes I fear I'll think something enough
times that it becomes true. So I consider
all the hours we spent undeniably alive:

Adolescent. Salt and milk and metal.
Elbow deep in the fire, bare backed,
unruly and unrepentant and unblinking.

Until the dream is just a splinter
in the hand that holds us. Significant,
until it isn't.

THE OLD DYKE TAKES ME TO MY FIRST GAY BAR

Shows me how to hold my back as straight
as I can manage someone like me someone
like us here in the dark under tongue of Soho
I'm seventeen and the air is wet with the women
in it shows me how to curve my mouth a little
how not to quiver when a hand finds itself just
above my secret palm flat against my skin
the old dyke looks like everyone in here has loved
her at some point lucky to have done so stained silk
under the low light knows how to breathe in time
to the music the old dyke doesn't flinch when
the world says she should outside the old dyke
shows me how to light a woman's cigarette
while it's still in her mouth passes down to me
a hundred ways of knowing without ever
having to ask her.

THE CHOIR

I could make this mean anything.
If there's a cure, let me have it —

the way the dance floor floods
with sunrise sometimes.

How I would roll my sleeves
up but there are still whole lives

under there, and you are still
beautiful. I am brushing a stranger's

hair off my shoulder, someone is
wearing your perfume. I am in reverse.

Everyone here is dancing the same
way those forty-nine people died.

If the knife kissed a little to the left,
we'd all be dead.

We hold our weddings where
we can also hold our wakes.

Call this ceremony, call this tradition
call this what it is.

Do you remember the oil fire,
the bath overrunning, how fast

you can un-hold a hand when you have to?
Wasn't this supposed to be beautiful?

My Therapist Says I Said

Search: define messiah

I am wiping down my insides with a Dettol cloth

    my sponsor says we cannot save anyone

I wear my Superwoman costume when I have sex

    have learned to avoid the biscuits at AA (always stale)

    and go for peppermint tea instead which is almost mouthwash

which is almost alcohol

I am hoovering the whole house, tending to the mirror with an old top,

tidying away all the newborns

Last night I caught a fox going through my rubbish so I broke its neck —

nobody takes from me, even things I do not want

In the morning I post my tongue to my mum's house alongside a note

instructing her to never give it back

When it isn't returned I bang my fists against the door, try and shout about my
    voice

    opening as wide as I can, a fleshed-out grapefruit, a hamper of silence

My mum upstairs gargling herself into the sink spitting

I'm sorry darling I'm sorry

I can't hear you

CHERUB

In what is neither a new nor radical act of being in love I try and imagine knowing you as a child.

There's that one photo of you in your kitchen, wrists fat and your face all cherub, all un-kissed and I imagine being what, six with you? The first night we spend together you tell me you fell in love at nine years old and you are so, so serious, in the dark, where I can hear you not smiling. When I was nine I wanted to be a news reporter or a chef or beautiful where instead I was dumpy and really, probably, if I was to know and love you as a child you would have to have bullied me, which would have been easy. Except I am forgetting when I was nine you were grown, growing, getting up from your knees and I want to say wait, wait, wait for me.

And you did.

Next of Kin

Didn't you tell me I was the favourite?
Fertile as a newly battered clock,
ripe as thick bleach? Our name is
a fishbone in my own throat.
I've always been good at making
things difficult — mixing up 'catastrophe'
with 'occasion' and so putting on the wrong
dress, forgetting to set the timer for dinner,
a persistent penchant for the perishable.
Wasn't it you who gave me an appetite
for impossible things? I want to be
as beautiful as I am angry, my own baby,
to slip into religion like a pair of second
hand shoes. In some ways I'm selfish —
holding up the queue at the buffet, unable
to decide. In others I am bone china
on the hardwood floor. Still waiting
on the slot machine jackpot.

EVEN THOUGH I WASN'T INVOLVED IN THE AFFAIR

it was still a cold penny pressed to the palm.
A secret that doesn't hurt you is barely a secret.
I was just learning a bird's breath language,
holding lemon sorbet on my tongue,
fashioning neutrality into a table cloth.

When the priest leaves confessional, is the walk
home longer? Does he wash his hands just for knowing
that knowing is its own kind of intimacy? Even though I
wasn't involved in the affair, I could give you a thousand
excuses. I could explain away the December heat.

I could make the dog walk on its two back legs.
I could break open the parentheses and watch
you cry with what's inside.

Then I would make you forgive her.

The Ways Women Speak to Each Other or Bonding Rituals for Mother/Daughter Pairings

Width of a stray hair on a black top.
The right mouth making the earth
a single passion fruit pip. The moon's
image (beautiful, unfathomably large)
which cannot be recalled on a whim
with any accuracy.

Aspartame daydreams. Salt swelling. A single ditch.

Some constant collection. A girl turned out
like a pocket — lint. Unvirginity. A pointed
cough over a rumbling stomach. The stillness
of tectonic plates. An agreement of peace.
The silent violence of fresh snow. A surgeon's
precision. White noise to sleep.

Bath water, boiled kettle, the faint hiss of reached capacity.

Needlepoint. Acrylic smell. Plastic
snapping. The pressure of entertaining.
Red cheeks. Blood on the porcelain.
Grooved hands from the gripping.
How they name lipsticks:
Silk Sunrise, Summer Moon, Serenade.

A dog's velvet, crushable skull in a manicured hand.

I

In the hospital
I'm trying to say goodbye
Throat tight and wordless.

POEM FOR MY BROTHER. AS IN:

Open-mouthed dream. Sweet as maple syrup and twice as difficult. Language is its own kind of cruelty and I want to invite you halfway to here. Listen, listen, listen — be the lounging lizard if you like. I'll be the hot tropic sun, the baked concrete slab beneath your belly. Keep bending if that's best. I'll break the rules for you, re-define speech until it's a silver noise settling in its sentiment. Soft-jawed superhero. I'll make the world play the incomprehensible one. We can bask in all you know and how you say it, jewelling the air. Tongue wet and perfect as jade.

It All Happens So Fast, Doesn't It?

One minute you are seeing which of you has enough cash

to buy tokens for the photo booth, seven years later she's dictating

funeral songs at the same station. She says Wild World,

by Cat Stevens, & not to listen to her mother,

who she says will try and get creative, face lit up with mischief

so you make a note in your phone: Wild World by Cat Stevens,

in case you forget, the chances of which would be pretty slim,

all things considered, in so far as that the first person

you have ever loved has cancer. It all happens so fast, doesn't it?

One minute you are bathing together, sitting on the toilet seat

watching her shave her arms, the next you are watching her

in the barbershop mirror, the clippers running without apology

over places on her that you've never seen

(which you thought, before this moment, was an impossible description),

the hairdresser waving her hands at the cash desk saying *no, no, no,*

honestly, it's fine. One minute you are young and open mouthed, the next

you're counting down from nine lives, remembering all the people

you have been together.

HONESTLY

The closer we are to one another the less space
we can collectively call ours — there is no use
drawing a map if it ends up the width of the world.
In another telling of this story I have learnt how
to have without having to hold but for now mostly
I am holding without having. Give me half the chance
to talk about myself and I will say something reprehensible

like yes, I am almost always thinking about love
or how I want to be described as 'arresting'
which is not something an arresting person
would say. 'Honestly' is probably my favourite
word even though it suggests I am often not telling
the truth until I announce that I am doing so,
but I don't think it's wrong to let people know

that you really mean something. What do we do
with all the tiny spaces between us when we are
lucky enough to witness them simultaneously?
To what extent would you say that you are living,
more so than that life is just happening to you?
If I hold out each hand, which are you taking?

Listen, I'm Just Saying

For the sake of scene setting:
seven churches burned. A beached whale.

Dreammoods.com tells me that some part of my subconscious
is giving birth to another.

If I had to choose, I'd say I always smell like sex
and hair dye and cocoa butter.

I break the week up into snortable chunks:
Google how to treat chemo fatigue, buy a new phone charger.

De-stoning the avocado makes me feel capable of doing something senseless.
I want to be the subject of an affair. Buy an overpriced coat.

Shave my armpits. You tell me you won't join the social programme
in case you make a friend who ends up dying

and I'm glad your illness hasn't robbed you of your pessimism,
infected you with an alien cheeriness, your wit lying dormant as a fat old dog.

Sometimes it's easier to imagine myself as an extra on a high-budget film set.
Over-salting food and avoiding nostalgia is the new self-care.

Listlessness is easy. If you really love someone, every poem
is romantic. Tell my psychiatrist I'm cured, please.

Call my brother. Tell him I love him.
I have so much being wrong left to do, as it happens.

It can be hard to keep track of what you have
when you acclimatise to the losing.

I can be transparent now — this new territory
affording me new honesty. I don't want to be.

If you pray to God hard enough
you'll get an out of office pointing you in the right direction.

HAVE
after Joan Larkin's 'Want'

I'm in the office offering up my name, you're in the kitchen
pressing the plates clean, rinsing the vegetables, sucking the salt
off. I'm in the armchair making my mouth small, stretching
my legs out, you're in the bedroom fussing the cotton.
We're in the bathroom, running the hot tap, naming our new
saints, delaying the evening. When the day doesn't interrupt,
you're teaching me to foxtrot, writing my stage directions,
catching the lemon pips. I'm laying it all out — lighting
a candle, curating a life, practicing future. You're right
there behind me, finding a place for it. I'm ready to give
up, putting the pen down, closing the book shut. You're
preparing patience. We're standing at the same view; I've got
my hands in the wet grass, you're watching the skyline,
we're shoulder to shoulder.

BREAD AND HONEY

In the morning I wade waist deep into the lake,
as far as I can go whilst allowing me enough time
to come back & double check you're just asleep —

haven't left, aren't leaving,
your chest still heaving with being.

One August, when we were little, you got
food poisoning, so we did nothing but eat
green apples & drink tap water,

the bones in your shoulder coming
up to kiss your brown summered skin.
It wasn't like I was taking care of you,

just that I witnessed you unstrong
(looked like a day going backwards)
& you knew no one would believe me.

Sometimes I make it a game.
See how many words I can make
from Host V Graft Disease
stem cell transplant.

All the blood inside of me is slow and forgiving.

Haven't you spent enough time surviving
surviving?

Now is the time for the soft body of bread
& honey.

Pollen fingered flicking through a future
where the fish in the mouth of the beast
has found its way back into clear water.

COMMUNAL GARDEN

A cousin who isn't a cousin not really is outside / barefoot on the concrete yelling something the house walls are eating up / you step outside / he has a toad in his hot June hands / the creature slick and throbbing like a removed heart / your cousin who is not your cousin / a tiny playground surgeon / his eyes full of excitement to touch something for the first time / nobody there to tell him no / turns just as you uncurl a single finger out to feel it / throws the creature from the balcony / his face fixed with glee / then walks back into the kitchen / does not turn around / not ten years later your cousin who is not your cousin not really / a tiny playground surgeon / still cannot get enough of that feeling / full of excitement to touch something for the first time / to tell him no is to say nothing at all / and when you lie down flat you are still young enough / that you become concave / a slow beat between the rib cage / like a toad / in two hot June hands

D Is for Dead — No — Dad.

All therapists' offices look the same,
same blue chair to stick to in the summer,
thighs young & unforgivable, same woman
sitting in front of you, same voice. Same school,
same training, same question,

'Dad?'

'Dead' & she says 'oh, desire' &
I say 'no, dead' & she says 'detriment'
'damaged' 'destructive' 'destroyed'
she says 'difficult?'

'Dead' & she says 'oh, denial' &
I say 'no, dead' & she says 'dull'
'declining' 'derailed' 'damned'
she says 'drowning?'

'Dead' & she says 'oh, directionless' &
I say 'no, dead' & she says 'different'
'devastating' 'dysfunctional' 'debilitating'
she says 'despairing?'

'Dead' & she says 'oh, dear.'

LIKE I SAID —
EVERYONE I LOVE IS CAPABLE OF DYING

When we find the mouse it is heavy-breathing by the pond in your garden

its two eyes glassy and reflecting everything's enormity

upstairs you tell me it would have died anyway

whether we made a bed for it or not

I just want to know if I drag myself to the water before I go

that someone will offer me the pink of their palm take me inside

or sit with me let it happen gently understand not all deaths are equal

your neck when I kiss it tell you I know is so salty and alive I almost

beg you not to go pretend for a second that this is how it is

that if we love someone enough we can condemn them to eternity

in a way that is forgivable preserve and pickle our favourite people

I know too many ghosts to believe it for longer than a second instead

hold your warm living face in my hands and ask you aren't we lucky

aren't we so so lucky

I'VE MADE A GHOST FLINCH BEFORE

Pork-belly-tongued
everything I have ever done
I did for someone else
slipping into selflessness
like a silk negligee
crying on the tube again
all that matters is I look
beautiful & remain regrettable
the last glass of celebratory champagne
caviar & food poisoning
for each man interested in me
I spend a pound of my own money
& this feels like reward
my mouth is always flooding
even when I am not hungry
sometimes I try to see how much I can hold
before I start to leak
a slow drip
a creeping stain on a cream ceiling
silly spill on a satin sash
say servile say cerebral seriously
say sacrifice with a straight face
say something about good sense
spare me all the stuttering
the summoning of strength

Etymology of Dyke

the joke starts with two girls smoking a cigarette

the safest way for their mouths to share a space

both of them returning home nicotine thick

on their fingers little intimacies close as a bird's feather to its breast

the joke starts with two girls closing their eyes when they dance

at one point I was underage even if I never felt it

disappearing my angles into warm red wine

becoming boundaryless in some sticky floored abyss

the joke starts with two girls on a nameless train

perfumed perched wet and sculpted as cliff face

knees barely touching each stranger a God

with its eyes open

the joke starts with two girls not saying anything

fruit fly escaping a pair of clapped hands

threats in peripheral vision are closer than they appear

milk curdling in an antique tea-cup

the joke starts with two women   walking into a bar

unsure of how not   to love one another

risk (noun): a situation involving   exposure to danger

two women walking into a bar   two women walking into a

joke starts with two women

never ends

Is That Glitter in Your Sweat?

Not sure how we made it here, both of us,

your pale shoulders pressed to my back

in their black leather harness, a prison

of your own choosing, your skin slick

to touch from the heat of body next

to body, body burning into

being what it should, all the men

in here are in love & not with us,

what a spectacle, to be present

& invisible all at once, all the

desire we were told was desolate

& derelict is ours now, delicious

& undamnable, in the smoking area

you shout to tell me last year scientists

concluded there is no single gay

gene, but a series of genetic variants

that each have a tiny effect on who

we are, like inside of us there is

an orchestra, & on the outside

we are dancing to our own music,

both of us, not sure how we made it here,

but understanding why it feels

so inevitable.

II

You meet me after.
The lift's full of the living.
A cruel irony.

MY UNCLE CAN'T DANCE

If you hold your fist like that you'll break your wrist
or your thumb come let's move through the day like
engine oil in the front seat of the car is a latke for you
the bag is going grey from white with the goodness of it

my uncle watches me take it apart with my hands so he
can be sure of at least one thing I've eaten today skinny
cunt he says fat bastard I reply steam rising when I laugh

my uncle is work-callused in summer the colour of old light leather
doesn't talk a lot but still has the presence of a boot through
a frozen lake all the birds fleeing their nests as it happens
my uncle can't dance but is always driving to somewhere

or back from it somehow never more than five minutes
away when I call all of him enormous and silent beside
me driving home from the hospital or therapy at the traffic
lights I make a brand new fist to show him
better, he says. Better.

A Series of Truths

If I think too hard about the fact you learnt
to fuck me like that from someone else I get upset

I stay in the bath until I'm wrinkled
because I want my back to be the first back
you've ever licked and I can't make it so

If I get out now I'll be upset with no right
& you'll be perfect in the kitchen light like marble if marble

were liquid each time you call me *greedy* your gums come
out the same shade secret flesh always is

pink as a new day and I know what you mean is
for me but I'm still going to pout about it

until you come over, hook your thumbs
round my waist suddenly

I'm vulnerable as an upturned fish
a salmon's soft underbelly

and for a second I can believe everyone else
was just a warm up a test run

that we simply had no time to waste
with each other.

Please Slam the Door on Your Way Out

Three black birds a rip in the sky.
When she dies, she's coming back

a sequinned thing. Spectacular.
Inconvenient. She'll be reincarnated

as the long hair on a long-haired
butch. She'll be the butcher's blade.

When she comes back, she's making
an entrance. She'll become occasion.

Serrated velvet. Beautiful
just for the hell of it.

Although the dying may be ordinary,
she'll be reborn as the fist against

the bathroom mirror.
Bethlehem burning before the birth.

LW, CW, GW

All my secrets are planning an intervention. In the fridge are forty-eight Slim Fasts. Strawberry flavoured. When I tell you they are out of date you say, 'That's what will make them so effective.' New app says I have a body fat percentage of a number smaller than my age. When the doctor asks if I have a history of family illnesses, I don't know how to mention the disappearing. How my sister went missing as a teenager and only just returned and we never talk about it. When I go home I feel like I'm tapping on the glass of my own life. 'Morning sickness was the best diet I've ever been on', you say. The doctor asks if there's anything that could have caused the weight loss. New app says I'm close to achieving my goal.

Rather Than Forgetting Her Voice

I eat powdered sugar from a tablespoon
drink condensed milk straight from the tin
like a cloudy sky filling my mouth
wave to wherever she is which I don't think
is up there or down below more like just behind me
close as the past ever is I let the sun kiss me
and I even kiss it back it's a miracle
we get to call anything ours so I hoard
all the goodness I can get my hands on
grind the day between my teeth and grin
at all my friends not only am I in love
but I'm the best at it I buy a dozen
roses for my girlfriend saying look! look
what I've done for you! and then the whole estate
is a picnic basket all the bus stops strawberry
punnets and I still haven't forgotten her voice.

This Is How It Will Go

When I imagine it it's late April
the sun a dried apricot drowning
us in orange light the day almost
leaving I'm making nervous shapes
with my hands the three of us lined
up like tenses the two of us in reality
making a mirror of the doorway
the kitchen table wherever else
great reunions happen

your breath will be so clean a window
I mistake for air I want to walk through
you'll ask about her my daughter she'd be
not quite me the same way I'm not quite you
but same jealous eyes same long nose
not the same thirst not the deep insatiability
a well refusing to fill no matter who carries
the water I'll explain best as I can how I
forfeited her couldn't bear the thought

of her finding me one day outside
when I should be in back on the wet
ground trying to turn the night into
something I can trade for daytime
but what about you I'll ask what
about you and you'll tell me how
long it has been put each chip on
the table and tell me easily
'It's not too late you know.'

I Am Sitting on the Tube Feeling like a Blood Cell Inside of London's Body

& thinking about your cancer. I want my potential for violence to overshadow my ability to commit it. Jubilee line announces Kilburn & I think about my first girlfriend & her mattress on the floor, the heat of her dogs, their bodies & ours, how their bites were never totally inconceivable. Always a season away from showing themselves & I want so badly to be the pink wet mouth of a feral thing. I think about my first girlfriend & how small we were, our school uniforms catching dog hairs and creases in the night, how we never kissed but knew we wanted to & how it was this unchangeable fact that allowed us to call ourselves together. I know she has a matching tattoo now with a woman she has been with for six months & I could laugh but honestly haven't we all been one good fuck away from saying actually, yeah, I will permanently alter my body with a reminder of yours and no, I won't promise not to regret it? When it first happened, when your body began being a body the wrong way, did you feel it? Sometimes, depending on where I'm going, C11 says Westcroft Way & I think about how we both existed once before we had the words for it, getting to the centre of the same lollies or summer bruising ourselves in the same way & how we were so reckless with our hatred, turning inward like reverse sunflowers. Knee-deep in the dirt we could have seen the stars if we wanted to, strained our necks upwards and admired it, the world's tablecloth, the silverware sparkling out of reach. How we thought there'd be a tomorrow to do it in.

A Little Amnesia

How many times can a story
repeat itself until they have
to get new actors in you aren't
allowed to break confidentiality
so you bring me to the source
nowadays you smell undone
like wet flour there is mascara
under your eyes for a second
you could be a bird trapped
in an oil spill rather than an
addict in a community centre
I want to be able to write
what saves you
I am building you a labyrinth
& drawing the map
too I'm asking you to follow me
know your way out
all the advice is at odds with each other
I'm supposed to love you into
pre-purge porcelain little
crystal figurine so polished
I can almost see myself in you
I'm supposed to leave long
enough you have to get sober
just to be sure that this is real.

THIS DYNAMIC IS OURS

I want your hand heavy with each thick

silver ring thin-fingered and faithful to find

my thigh hold me close as a well-deserved

win I want the men on the tube carriage

across the bar eyeing us up from the comfort

of themselves to know you could end it all

in a second but it would ruin your good white

shirt I want to spend the evening steeped

in your tenderness spilling outside the lines

of each other lover I learnt to love you some

other life ago so if I am good at any single thing

let it be this settling into the hard nook of your

arm being yours and nothing else matters

even when it feels like a knife edge we're

dancing on all I ever have to do is look down

and see us in it

smiling.

HEREDITARY

Technically, I can't help it. Hold me up there,
where the sun hits, and you can see it. Another year
cracking open, an empty Russian doll inside of it. I tried
to rid myself of what they gave me — their want, the dire
need and all it called for. What's a family name but a thread
you can't cut? I thought I could outsmart our genes, third
generation lucky. I thought I could outrun them, got ready
for the long stretch. If I cup my hands to my ear, I can almost hear
us beginning. Even now I succumb to thinking I can still ride
this one out. Buy a new passport. Shave off all my hair.
When people talk about the missing girl, I'll say I haven't heard.

'THEY CAN BUN MY FLESH, BUT THEY CAN'T TOUCH MY SPIRIT'

referencing J Hus - 'Spirit'
for Sadie, Talia, and Pembe Tosun

No small part of you has ever managed to be insignificant —

so while with the others it is the removal of something tangible:

a new-born baby, a tangerine-sized heartache,

something they can shrink right down,

eye coming away from the microscope

how remarkable, incredible,

drunk on comparison

    (*'they are threading a needle through my veins all the way into my heart'*)

it makes sense that none of you is sacrifice-able.

This is how I justify it. Because I want it to be easy.

I want it to be so easy we laugh about it —

your eyebrow raised in the face of it, your teeth clean from kissing them

it's almost like they don't know who you are, blood

drawn is doing the needle a favour;

stubbornness begat survival so blessed be

those on the receiving end of your screw face.

    (*'they are drilling straight into my bone'*)

It's almost like they don't know who you are.

What's a little bit of struggle when to make it is your mother tongue?

When you are Sadie-is-my-mother strong?

It's impossible to marry you to this disease

when the idea of you weak is wholly wrong.

It's almost like they don't know who you are;

still catching sunlight in your clenched fists.

North London princess.

Have you ever seen a cherry blossom storm in Tottenham?

The sun setting behind the Asda in Edmonton?

Beautiful in all your grit. Not in spite of it.

They can bun your flesh — but they can't touch your spirit.

Who Can I Blame for the Legs That I Have?

DNA test confirms you are ninety-eight percent Irish,
two percent Northern European. It does not tell you
who felt the grape split under their bare foot first.
Cannot trace the wine back to its bloodline,
bring you a great great grandmother held like a baby,
swaddled in origin. All our women are midwifing,
at wakes, tending to excuses.

There are things about you I cannot stop:
a bruise spreading wrist to elbow,
fresh ink on the page of the body.
The folded corners of sobriety —
how the blood embraces the cotton,
the catholicism of alcoholism.
Our own children cannot prevent us

from becoming our mothers.

III

Falling in love stood
In the sleepless chamber of

grief — a strange gift.

WE NO LONGER KNOW EACH OTHER

but I've the eczema to prove we once did,
though I've been trying my best to treat
it. When people ask, I give you the life
you deserve. Oh, her? Thriving orchid
flower now! Home in some sweet-aired green
house. English teacher. Haven't seen her
in ages, actually, but I know recently
she was reading poems, baking bread,
not needing to get sober. Folding herself
into a community garden, growing old with
hymnal grace, a permanent state of sweet
reminiscence. Yeah she's pretty busy having
friends, keeping up with them. Charity work.
Last time I went round she'd made the table
up for dinner, which was sweet but I couldn't
stay. That's how it is with us, still finding
time to love each other but mostly busy,
mostly her, you know? When the doctor sends me
for the X-ray, says my lungs may be full of fluid
or empty as a breath-filled balloon, I almost
call you up.

ROSEWATER

Each time I come back up
rosewater drenched thankful
I swear I would become another drowned thing
for you if you wanted me to

our hands wringing the prayer
from the silk both of us catching
the light winter warm
worship looking like two women

trying to become ghosts two ghosts
trying to become women
broken boned giddiness

all that
pleasure so permissionless

PAINTING THE DAY BY NUMBERS

I eat the acrylics making my tongue
alizarin crimson instead of just red
like a tiny celebration in my mouth
& continue my day cutting the poem
into couplets & checking my spam folder
that is full of beautiful women who want
me to show them my cock someone I knew
as a baby but not for much longer posts
on Facebook that in Queens New York
they are currently keeping a refrigerated
van outside Elmhurst Hospital for the dead
which leads me to wonder where you are
right now if you're cold whether your skin
is a different shade than I knew it maybe
phthalocyanine blue or *payne's grey*
I hope afterwards we still recognise
each other or maybe wear name tags
so I can find you easily our embrace
soft as it's ever been your face so nearly
unchanged & when I am done with this
train of thought I go back to the house
asking all its chores of me pour the water
from the vase because the flowers have
already died which would be fine but
I only bought them yesterday
and that just doesn't seem fair.

WHATEVER IS LEFT IN THE PACKET

it is best to learn death early on —
if you wean a baby on chilli seeds,
by the time there is a word
for burning they have no use
for it. all their teeth growing
into a wet marsh mouth.
it is possible to be too young
for a funeral, your fat
tiny hands a bird's hungry
beak, distracting all the mourning
mothers, but old enough for death
to visit, take great love from its
unmade bed.

SOMEWHERE ALL THE OTHER GODS ARE LAUGHING AT US

but if we don't pray who will?
nowadays our poems are less
like poems, more just statements
of fact. if you say something enough
it becomes truth. 1) your name was
not your name until your mother
said it so & watched you dance
to it. 2) our hands can hide the sun

yes, even from down here

can protect our pale faces.
these tiny things, our personal
planets. maybe holy is what you
need, so we will resurrect the church.
measure the space from miracle
to miracle. in my next life
I am coming back to you
slow as sugar water.

spark of small joy. body of the banyan tree.

I'm Pretty Busy

looking up my dead friend on facebook.
my ex-girlfriend's ex-girlfriend's new girlfriend
looks beautifully familiar.

going to the same bar as when i was seventeen
and promising i never would again.
dancing to new songs.
folding origami swans
across the room with someone
who could be lovable if i let them.
getting vex. letting my face set
like this so no one moves to me.
not believing my mum when she says
she's sober. giving up smoking.
getting neurotic about wrinkles.
eating salads. getting neurotic
about skin collagen & weight loss &
also weight gain. washing my hair
every other day. convincing myself
i can stop anytime i want to.
buying new toothbrushes. arriving
at my appointments fifteen minutes early.

the last time i saw my dead friend, men smashed
the stained glass above her front door until each shard
was cellulite in the thigh of movement,
the moment becoming a rabbit's snapped neck.

when impulse slips its tongue in?
not biting. getting out of the car
when i hit the deer, when the sky
is baby pink & making a nursery
of the scene below it. taking the bait
when it's best to.

looking up my ex-girlfriend's ex-girlfriend's
new girlfriend on facebook.
my dead friend looks beautifully familiar.

Gay Chicken, Actually

young, and without the right processes for desire,

every gathering inevitably resulted in a game of Chicken.

a test of nerve. who could get closest to the other

before bottling. I was the best. the bravest. met the lips

of each friend unflinching, their laughter splitting the evening wide

open. safe in the permission of symmetry, I became a place

to place wanting.

(I was always brushing their hair but cutting my own.)

every dare sent in my direction until our bodies outgrew

the excuses we'd given them. so we tried on new

disguises: it's not what you think. girls are different.

we can do this with each other.

Wearing My Bargain Best

Mumma says you must really trust
someone to let them hurt you like that.
To tell you the truth, I'm in fishnets

underneath all my clothes,
a Poundland honey-trap.
What is the suffix for female

suffering? I'm asking to be
bent over somewhere.
I can see myself being

seen, I can see all my ribs
like this it's been a long
time coming. I am swollen

as a blood clotted limb.
If I asked you really nicely
would you bring me home?

Inside I am bleach-white.
I promise I am many things
before I am a woman.

I wouldn't want you worrying.

I Don't Know the Word for the Feeling Felt When You Think You Spot Someone You Know

before remembering that they're dead

wasn't that you just this evening
face screwed up all lemon
mouthed gold toothed
walking like you had somewhere
to be not gone
everyone's personal sunshine

could have sworn I saw you
arm round an anonymous waist
winking at no one in particular
the whole world gravitating
towards you as though a plug
had been pulled
almost ran to catch up
before I felt my face against the glass
blackbird going beak first for what
it wants the world letting it know
how that hurts

What We Are Given

A small pot and a plant to keep alive in it. South facing windows. Hot tarmac in the summer. Sweetcorn straight from the tin. Bone aching pain and then morphine. Sex that makes the backs of our knees sweaty. Betting shops. First kisses. Buses with wet top deck windows. Crying in public. Two magpies, for joy. Languages we don't speak. Loads of them. Prayers that feel too easy to say. Crisp sandwiches. Airplane seats with a kicking kid behind them. Recipes for yellow rice, apple cake, mac and cheese. Small pride. Postcodes. Patience. Prescriptions. Perseverance. Pensions. Peppercorns. Petulance. The alphabet. Grief, its moth dust on our fingers. Pick & Mix. Twelve step fellowships. Faithfulness. Chlorine in our eyes. Hot baths. Half time. Stomach pumps. Chemotherapy. Valentine's Day. Mathematics. Faithlessness. Impossible things. Words for other words when the other words just won't do. Birthday parties. Departure lounges. Yearning. Museums. Bathroom haircuts. Prime numbers. Numbing cream. Sports teams. Poetry. One for sorrow. Terms of reference. Fetishes. Traffic jams. Second chances. Jazz bands. Laboratories. Labradors. Lesbians. A little life in which to say 'We all love you so much. You can go now. It's okay.'

ACKNOWLEDGMENTS

Endless gratitude to my family.

Thanks to Kit Sinclair. For each time you sat at the end of the bed and said, 'read it to me.' For being my muse even when you don't realise it.

Thanks to Sadie Tosun. For raising an absolute phoenix of a daughter, without whom many of these poems would not have been possible.

Thank you to Out-Spoken Press, Barbican Young Poets programme and Apples and Snakes.

Thank you to Fern Angel Beattie and Write Bloody UK for taking a chance and publishing *What We Are Given*, my first full length collection. I am grateful beyond words.

Thanks to Talia Tosun. For never letting a draft go unlooked at. For everything you are and everything you continue to be to those who love you.

Special thanks to Angel Donor, Sohrab Mehta.

About the Author

OLLIE O'NEILL is a poet and writer from London, England. Aged 18, she won the National Youth Slam Championship and has since performed at venues such as The Royal Festival Hall, The Institute of Contemporary Art and Soho Theatre, as well as Cheltenham Literature Festival, Bradford Literature Festival, and Wilderness Festival. In 2019, her debut pamphlet *Ways of Coping* was published by Out-Spoken Press, exploring the relationship between misogyny and psychiatry.

IF YOU LIKE OLLIE O'NEILL, OLLIE LIKES...

Floating, Brilliant, Gone
Franny Choi

Drive Here and Devastate Me
Megan Falley

Pansy
Andrea Gibson

In the Pockets of Small Gods
Anis Mojgani

Bloody beautiful poetry books.

Write Bloody UK is an independent poetry publisher passionate
about bringing the voices of UK poets to the masses.
Trailing after Write Bloody Publishing (US) and
Write Bloody North (Canada), we are committed to
handling the creation, distribution and marketing of our authors;
binding their words in beautiful, velvety-to-the-touch books
and touring loudly with them through UK cities.

Support independent authors, artists, and presses.

Want to know more about Write Bloody UK books, authors, and events?
Join our mailing list at

www.writebloodyuk.co.uk

9 781838 033200